Write a Story

by

Verlena Sexton-Walker

authorHOUSE™

1663 LIBERTY DRIVE, SUITE 200
BLOOMINGTON, INDIANA 47403
(800) 839-8640
WWW.AUTHORHOUSE.COM

First published by AuthorHouse 09/28/04

ISBN: 1-4184-9588-3 (sc)

Printed in the United States of America
Bloomington, Indiana

This book is printed on acid-free paper.

Poems

IN RESPONSE

SURVIVING TO STRIVE
LIVING TO STAY ALIVE
STRIVING TO SURVIVE
THEY WANT ME TO SEE THROUGH TUPAC EYES
WHEN I AM COUNTING THE DAYS UNTIL I DIE

THE FILE IN THE BEDROOM
THE LADY ON THE STREETS SWIPING WITH A BROOM
IN RESPONSE TO THE STILLNESS
THAT WILL TAKE OVER THE BODY SOON

I AM LIVING TO STAY ALIVE
STRIVING TO SURVIVE
I AM CONSTANT TO MY EXPRESSION
NO TEARS IN MY EYES

THE MUSIC IS PLAYING IN MY LIVING ROOM
WHEN THIS IS NOT A NEGRO MOVEMENT
WILL I BE GONE SOON
MANY PEOPLE WANT ME TO ASSUME ANOTHER'S
IDENTITY
WHEN GOD CREATED ME NOT PERFECT BUT A DESTINY

IF I LISTEN TO WHAT IS PLAYING IN THE AIR INSIDE
IT BEGINS TO PLAY AROUND - NOT IN MY EYES
WHAT I HAVE CAN NOT BE SHARED WITH ANOTHER
HUMAN BEING

Verlena Sexton-Walker

WHEN OLD MEN CONTINUE TO LIE ABOUT WHAT THEY DREAM

SURVIVING TO STRIVE
LIVING TO DIE
THE HATRED IN THAT MAN EYES COME FROM MINE
ANOTHER'S IDENTITY CAN NOT BE ACQUIRED
IN A ROOM FILLED WITH WHITES AND NEGROES
TRYING TO TURN BACK THE HANDS OF TIME

ABSENT OF MALICE: MALICIOUS INTENT

Absent of malice
As I began to groom
The man of my life leaving the room
In which he states that all is good
Maybe you will give me some soon

Malicious intent is all that is understood
Closing the door of my bedroom

Absent of malice
The arguments never leave
As I began to press the shirt sleeve
This is the love that I must show
As the hatred overflows

Malicious intent is understood
By the slap of the hand
And the statement, "It's still good"
Absent of malice
Is all that is known
Out of place now
The thrill is gone
When the skin can not be torn

Malicious intent is what is meant
In the presence of misfits
To complicate idiots that think saying idiosyncrasy by
        a bitch that pants for this
Is within fear that exist

Absent of malice - Malicious intent
Is sex with a man that gives you a hint
That all he wants is his dick wet
Through dry salt meat that does that

I'LL CRY IN THE MORNING

When you search for love

Look into the eyes

This love that despairs as well as despise

When you are hurting

Please don't cry

Intertwine your eyes with mine

I love with a passion as strong as desire

I can not relate why

This is the love I share with you in my eyes

When you want company of the compassionate kind

Turn around and ask for mine

This is all that needs to be done

Have you not realize I am the only one

My eyes tell stories of love that is great

In Michigan this is call deterring hate

Master of deception I can conceive

Look in my eyes

AND

Believe

Justice within me

HOWEVER

When in need do not hesitate

This deploys hate

The rebirth of a mistake

OR

A fool life at stake

Not mines for heaven sake

PANAMONIA THING

My daughter
My sons
My two boys
My one girl
Is all I have left in this world
Mankind has succeeded
In defeating me

In the game of love
The tears in my eyes
Are tears of sadness
Are tears of joy
The tears in my eyes
Says no more

My father
My mother
My sisters
My brothers
Is nobody in my life now
You all know why
This family tree is not mine

These tears make my eyes shine
Are tears of happiness
Are tears of joy
These tears in my eyes
Says please no more

My friend
My cousin
My niece
My nephew
Are all part of this family
Not meant for me
True signs of victory

THE FRUSTRATION OF A 'WORKING' WOMAN

Divorce, I should be
That man didn't care a damn thing about me
He beat me constantly
With three babies
Became obscenity

A nine year old girl
In an abnormal psyche scene
A room full of old men after school
Telling all they had to do
Asking, "Who are you"
Closing the door
Saying, "She knows"

Baby girl sitting on the couch
Sick with the pneumonia
Key turns in the door
Crying, "I'm home, I want you"

Arriving without medicine for the little one
Nor shoes for her feet
Ready to make love
Yesterday, beat me

A nine year old boy
In an abnormal psyche scene
Trying to fulfill a dream
Of something that was not meant to be

Our boys are playing in the yard
Coming in the house stomping his feet
Raising his had to slap me
Gun goes off silently
911, call the police

Murder in self-defense
A middle school child
Stands along
Not knowing but knowing all along
Old bitches and young men
Are the episode
While he backups from a asshole

Rich man to a man with money
Tits never wrinkling
Country is honey
Called Yolanda
DOG TIT THAT
On the telephone
This is victory that never grows cold

Children in school
In abnormal psyche room
Shows what is between the lines
As I read what is on mine

"It is said that there are seven women for each and every man." (Verlena Sexton-Walker)

INAPPROPRIATE

This right here belongs to 'whom'
This right here belongs to you
This right here does not belong to damn fools

Inappropriate stands in a room

This right there is just for 'whom'
This right there is just for you
This right there is not just for damn fools

Inappropriate stands in my room

That there is not to be possessed
That there is not to be obsessed
That there is beauty in place
That there is directly in your damn face

Inappropriate stands on gravel outside
Saying you are pop time after time

Funny how exact we are
Turning, eyes afar…

Inappropriate drives away
With nothing more to say

At the exact time
Everyday….

THE CONCEPT

Trying to be a man
Trying to take a stand
Finding only a woman without a man
In this fuck-up world I live in

Snot, Knot, What am I not
Is the rhyme within the words
This only applies to a girl
That has not been heard

When I hear music, lyrics of a song
I began to think of a poem
That does not flip from the words
But is original and unique
As I recite it; as I speak

So much anger and hatred surrounds me
Because of this magnificent gift
Jealous lacking myth
This is the ending of what is seen as well as heard
Sorrow of drum majorette, ignorance of sport jock, and
                        band performance
These are elements of what is true and what is not
Being beautiful is all that is known
Fantasy is the foreseen
This is how a damned man dreams

A WAY OF LIFE

See me for what I am and not what you want me to be
Believe in me through the things I have done and not
through my family
Ask me to fulfill your wants because of your needs and
not because of greed
This is how your life proceeds…

A Way of Life is in the mist
As you snatch money from an old woman fist

Admiration
Build   are words of deep meaning
Send
Give   in which expression is voiced
This is how we began to make a chose

Build me a mansion on a hill for the love you feel
Reality in truth will keep it real
This way of life is how we will proceed
Tallying all wrongful deeds
Crucial is the course and action of choose
That man must not realize
Recognition of who you are than can not be criticize
Individuals of a specified domain
No one to take the blame

A Way of Life is the process that is put to test

Braid the hair; pull it back from the face
Let them know who is in the place
As they throw paper across the room
This is episodic to a teacher in school
A Way of Life is then the livelihood of damn fools
Detroit, Michigan has been finally used.

Waste of Enabilities

To live without one leg
While comatose in bed
With bugs jumping from your [my] head
Is an ideology of ill
That has no love to give

All-in-One is the thing
That can ruin everything
Is that the end
Or how we begin

To curse constantly
To swear continuous
Is waking from a nightmare
With mess-up hair

All-in-One is the thing
That can ruin everything
Is that the end
Or how we begin

To see everything as green
To always scheme
Is a fools game
That has no means

All-in-One is the thing

That can ruin everything

Is that the end

Or how we begin

This is the strife of an incognito man [woman]

Idolize

My eyes are hazel brown

My hair is honey blond

My lips are colored red

While I swing my feet from my bed

And all they seem to know

Is how to make me grow [glow]

My mind has many ideas

That only I can concept

The whiteness of my teeth

While I speak

What is apparent

Is my disgust

While they front

Description of who I am not

But who they want to be

And all they seem to know

Is my certain victory

This is my effervescent; sheer existence and all that

matters

My eyes intense in this pretense of who I should be

and

not who I am

And all that is apparent

Is who is damn

Write a Story

A family tree:

Martha is her name she stands with no man

Menis White is her brother

They do not have the same father or mother

Abigail Stewart cousin to both continuously looks for

hope

Of unity in this family; a bloodline not in the roots

This is said to be true

Constant Johnson descendants of above

Begins to trace her [family] history

How many people can be documented

She can't find any

Johnny Smith is the man to help all reunite

These are family members

You know why…

Martha, Menis, Abigail, Constant, and Johnny are all from an

adopted sequence of 100 years of mistakes

Let's develop the hate:

Martha was given to a Uncle whom rape her time and

time again

Abigail had a very good upbringing

Constant is the daughter of Abigail

John is Abigail husband

Bloodline getting closer…

Martha and Menis has the same father and mother
Menis is Abigail brother
Bloodline rooted…

Confusion over whom is kin
Incest is the ending
Ancestors to Constant family
Tainted, painted, undaunted…

Unusual; but true
No longer confused

As the story unfolds
Abigail is told all her children will be born with a
birth defect
Lacking self-respect
She does not understand
That she now belongs to every man
Married to John
Having five children
All with a known mental disorder

Abigail is Aunt Bella

Aunt Bella

Thoughts of sadness crosses the mind
Moments in time
Of life that is not grand
In the face of a woman
That is the oldness of the plan

Aunt Bella is the name
She has had many men
The bitch of Mississippi
Not knowing a status quo
How can this whore
Of everyone's brother

Going through trouble
Loving no one
As she turns to women
To be someone
The whore is a dike
Not an act
As she open her legs
Night after night

Aunt Bella
What is wrong
Is the age to old
Or is it still clothes
As a dick enters your pussy hole

Sadness is said to be eliminated through fucking

As she suck dick, disease

As she begins to lick

Aunt Bella is seventy now

Still trying to stay young

As she goes from rich to bum

Verlena Sexton-Walker

A Reunion

Congratulation, in celebration of a remembrance
This is a moment in time as we reminisce
Children playing
People saying, "Hi, Hello"
As the day becomes old

The sun is dying
Martha's baby crying
Jane walks away
With nothing more to say

Hallelujah, Praise Amen
As we depict again and again
Why did Sam leave Mary
Did Jerry become melancholy
These are people in a town that surrounds a sea

The still of night becomes salient
Music plays in effervescent
Emma disturbs the sequence
Shouting, "Who is this"
As Philip leaves the milieu

Hoop, Hoop, Array
The close of a wonderful exciting day
As green becomes gray
Why try so hard anyway

The Heritage

As he sits on the floor

Looking so hopeless

He begins to plot a plan that does not make sense

Room by room

He does not know how to choose

As he constantly gets used

This man is damn by a power greater than him

What is his destiny…

I suck dicks everyday

Licking pussy every night

This is my way of life

Basketball is my favorite sports

My colors are red with black shorts

How many times I am exploited

Does not matter

The money is good hour after hour

I only do it for a living

The commissioner has no mix feelings

I am 6'6' with a shaved head

But I am real freaky in bed

Do I seem mislead

They dare me to be intelligent

I admit I am scared

To much money to give-up

Shot the ball that's enough

Do you think I am being fuck

The heritage is the thing
This man is still playing games

TRIBAL QUEEN VERLENZA

She the image of a 'Tribal' Queen
Potency known
Her mind is complex
Her emotions are never shown
She stands with eloquence of tomorrows not lived
The future is foreseen
This is her heritage

'Tribal' Queen you are beautiful
Being righteous in stance
That's only your choose

Many try to overthrow her
Many try to deceive her
She stands along
Not with anyone
Never to mislead her
Wisdom and knowledge is in her existence
The destiny of an outcome
As she deploy a final victory
The accomplishment of onefulness
Creating history

Her name is 'Tribal' Queen Verlenza
She is a 'tribal' queen
This is her life foreseen
By whites, blacks, and all races

Why is she hated
Because she chooses herself an no one else
Not having a true sister or brother
A mistake in this life time has been made by her mother
Lacking regrets
This is 'Tribal' Queen Verlenza

Untouched…
Around male apes
Jealousy is the focus of old
As professional athletes insert there dicks in each and every old
asshole

'Tribal' Queen Verlenza foreseen this
'Tribal' Queen Verlenza knew this
'Tribal' Queen Verlenza is a living witness

Culture; ethnicity; identity; tradition; the heritage

ALIAS TONY WALKER

HELLO, the battery is on the floor
DID the car start
OF course not

HOW many times do we not react
TO a mental attack

SOMEONE took the battery out
WE were unaware
THE battery is on the floor
CLOSE the door

TWICE this has happen
DO we respond
TO a senseless individual
THAT is really a bum known as Von

TAKE the battery and start the car
DO you have to walk far
YOU left it in the yard
BESIDE a vacant truck
HOW many dicks did you suck
BEFORE you discovered you where fuck

IS this the last time you are mental attack
BEFORE you react

THE battery is yours to keep
IS it men or women you creep

MI

To do it again
Is to take a chance at losing
Before you decide, you must realize
That I know
This time you will lose
Continue chose the same
                Again
The shame is between your legs
While in bed desiring what you can not have
Don't feel bad or sad
This is the last time you can get a shot at this ass

Men of young from my generation
Did you hesitate
Now you procrastinate in your mistake
I am not a Negro but you continue to hate
Damn yourself
Fuck who else
This is your error, no more help

ELOQUENCE

You did her…

I am sorry
All I have to give is me
I'll make love to you
I'll caress you
I'll touch you gently
I'll give you me

You did him…

What is an apology
I gave you me
I open my legs passionately
As you kiss me
This is my apology
I gave you me

Leave me…

But I love you
And your fooliness
I can't leave you like this
My love is true
Not a pretense
Not trying to make sense

Verlena Sexton-Walker

Finally…

I gave you me
Provided you with love
Gave you two boys and a girl
Only thing is
Your condition
You didn't mention on our first date
This is why I hate
However, I do love you
Expression in words

ELOQUENCE

GPD

GPD is the sorriest ass police in history
They can't patrol the streets without fucking with me
Is it the blood I bleed
I'll provide them with the maxi pad off the ass
Claiming the victory

The 9th precinct is the picture show
Patrolling Gratiot Avenue
Old bitches are they game
Depicting a shame
I gave them the maxi pads from between the legs
So I can get the last laugh

How do young men of today
Throw they life away on old ass
Forget they youth and generation
Without hesitation

Standing in a environment force
Is a woman and a man
Holding hands
Raising her dress
The pussy swaddle the dick
The man is twenty-three and the woman is sixty-six
She salivates at the mouth with no teeth
This woman is a school superintendent
He is a pro athlete

What lesson does this teach
That it is giving nothing but a wet ass and false history

Jealousy is spoken in a conversation
Only thing is left is procrastination
Why would fucking old women bring the green eyed
                    monster
It does not; only aging disease and a disease cock
This is not nasty in words
This is not a rumor heard
This is a boy trying to hurt a girl
            That doesn't care if he drops dead out of this
                    motherfucking world

Now you been told
Fuck old
Never to know the difference in jealousy, lust, or desire
Why continue to tide her
GPD says she is nobody

NOTHING

The ideal is that whom we are is whom we want to be
This could be nothing…

"I am very prosperous" says a man
"I can have any woman
I prefer the very old
I am twenty-one I'm told
My destiny is to marry at sixty-three
By than I will be famous"

Nothing is the dick hanging
Nothing is the g-string swinging
Nothing is a man playing games
That he lives without shame

The woman believes she is somebody
Because of her job
Her career is not hard
She fucks unthinkingly
Of the image she is giving
This is what she calls her power
As she fucks nobody

Nothing is the wet dick head
The old ass you having lying in your bed
Wasting your money on a town of misfits
Over certain bull shit
This is that nothing that thinks he is all that

33

PLACE SETTING

First of all; I left you all
First of all; I did not chose y'all
Most of all; love is in reverse
                    Did that hurt

Men and women surrounding me as I elevate
Through speech and gesture of episodic scenes
While they focus on how to hate

Second are the lights
First is the electricity
Second is the gas
First is the crap in the ass

Men and women standing tall
Waiting for her to fall
As she walks down the hall

My first cousin is a retard
She does things that are not very smart
No hair; she wears a wig
As she begins to sing
This is how she says she stays sane…

Finally, place a dish
Because I am tired of this bullshit

MOVEMENT OF CIVILIZATION

Why would citizen award me
They have the victory
The Philippines is the City
Not Greenville, Mississippi
Many are mislead
By whom I am
The game is to best me
Through the stupidity of man

The Master Degree was received in Detroit
Not the heart of Mississippi
Whom cares what GPD does
They don't really scare me

Standing in the walls
Is a psychotic male bitch
He don't know his ass from his shit
He talks retarded to me over and over again
This is how he believes he will win

The PH.D. is on the horizon
This is the truth not a lie
That is why they ask, "If you had wings would you fly"

Walking through a church, a man is confused
Is he on a mission or being used
White men will never tell him what is true

Verlena Sexton-Walker

He is subjected to continuance abuse

These are the ignorant idiots that lived through a
                              movement of civilization
That is not epistemology
Old folks will never be able to claim any this victory
Fucking young should be history
                              With regards to me
Fuck 'cause you want the piece of meat

The Concept of God

I am God

I am Almighty

I am what you believe in

To make your life brighter

I create personalities

Which should you be…

Hippest

Thuggish

Masculinity

The concept of God is brought about

By people whom is looking for away out

That believes that they have created a holy environment

This concept of God is well meant

Let me see…

Do you want to be me

I am alrighteousness

I am spirituality

I am make-believe

To acquire me

It does not take money

Only your mind and soul that leaves the body

I create convicts

That believe they are not criminals

As they unfold a scheme

This is how a man begins to dream

The concept of God is brought out
By misfits and have nots'
Standing on a mountain top
Thinking about all they got

In essence…
The personality of strength I create
The personality of wisdom and knowledge is not at stake
 The personality of culture, ethnicity, and identity is
                        all in one
Which should you be…
An Evangelist
A misfit
A concept
Or all that is left
 A person with a life biography that is destiny in the
                        making

I am God
I am Almighty
I am your certain victory_
THIS CONCEPT OF GOD LIVES IN THE {ME}

Utilizing a Tool

A male psychotic bitch

Driving his sister Mazda 626

Drops my mammy off at her residence

Looks at me and says, "You make me sick

You a big crazy bitch

Your children are past tense"

In my Cadillac Seville

I look at him and say "You're in overkill

Thanks for the blessings

Raise the sister and brothers

You are their father; they have no other"

Alias Tony Walker is the man

With a dominant plan

He waves his hand

Saying, "Of course, I'll win"

I turn my head, "This man is playing"

He can't read or write

He does not know how to spend money right

He is not wrap to tight

The children are utilize for pain, gain, and fame

He can hardly pronounce their name

This is not a game

My memory is altogether now

I know why

The attitude; the personality; the shoes

This man I will continue to use

Alias Tony Walker is his name

He has a faulty plan

Continuing the confusion

He believes he has won

When life is promise to no one

SHARE THE LOVE - LOSE THE LIFE

Spread me thin
You can't win
Share the love
Lose the life
This is how you develop strife
Monopolizing is just not right
These are all struggles in life

An eighteen year old girl stomach protrudes
She has gotten pregnant before she finishes school
Not knowing what to do
She is subjected to continuance abuse
Pacing the sidewalk without shoes
She turns and says, "First I have to finish school"

Share the love
Lose the life
A sign of being unwrapped
Monopolizing becomes right
These are consistencies in life

Matthew is a handsome man
Is goal oriented
His life he plans
Standing in a coffee shop
He begins to talk

"I'll hit the lottery one day," he says
He just did
Though the victory of a card

Spread me thin
Will you win
Share the love
Lose a life
This is to deploy strife
Monopoly of a person is just not right
These are consistencies and struggles in life
SHARE THE LOVE; LOSE THE LIFE

The Lies and The Tries
{The Reality of your Mentality
is that once done; remain done}

Open up brother and tell me something…
How do you think the words that comes from your ink shames me
How do you think what you document frames me
How do you think what you say and do defrayment me
An entity of a government development of hate in mist of a
mistake

They said I took a cookie from my baby and beat him in the face
I live in a house that was a dilapidated disgrace
No food or beverage to been seen in the place
My children went to school in rackety clothing and shoes each and
everyday
This is an entity of the government way of hate in mist of deceit
that places everyone at stake

Telephone rings as I rise from my bed
My eyes crosses in my head
The Social Worker told me my children could never come home
As I hung up the phone
This entity of the government is not smart
Why do they try so hard

Abandonment of all three is said to be done by me
As I leave Mississippi

43

My husband knows my whereabouts

He has just as much responsibility as me

To raise these three

This entity of the government is the disgrace as they suck dick and

eat shit everyday

The doctor, lawyer, educator, pro athlete, etc... mistake

This entity of the government will pay

{The Reality of your Mentality is that once done; remain done}

Immobilize the Obvious

Victimization

Violation

Discrimination

These are the words of an ignorant nation

That jealousy controls

This is what I know and not told

I stand alone

Waiting on them to fuck up

The hopeless bunch use a mental preference

That is an expression of idiots

These are the misfits

Lack of fear

Lack of care

Don't give a damn

As this man takes the same stand

I stand by myself

Patiently…

Drastic measures will be taken

As this man and his environment have mistaken what is evident

You took damn and gave spirit

You took curse and gave a blessing

You took family and gave an identity [through ethnicity]

Lacking blackness of a race

This man does not hesitate in his mistakes
 No one can change who I am only to change they self-respect and
        what they call a man
Are you still so readily to shake a hand
While you continue to take the same damn stand
Who is the blame
You the one that should be shame

GIVE ME THAT

How can I sustain the pain?…
When I am in a country where I don't have to relate to any man…

From my titty nipples; in my stomach; through my vagina
I feel desire constantly
This is the pain that lives in me
A blissful feeling with misgivings
Is this what I want
I don't believe so
As someone violates me once more
Say, "Baby I want you"
Say, "Baby I need you"
Say, "Baby I can't live without you"

A victim not of society but within mentality
The reality stands tall
As he lies in the carpet in my bedroom next to the backdoor hall
This man lacks sanity when he thinks he is my property
Why does he want to possess me
He Said, "Baby I want you"
He Said, "Baby I need you"
He Said, "Baby I can't live without you"

The feeling begins in my titts centers my stomach remains in my slit
Transcending in black is a lifeless figure that is not tangible to the touch
He expresses so much

One thing for sure is the cure of knowing that this is his only
[chose] - only [recourse]
A lifeless figure that never uses his voice...
Say, "Baby I want you"
Say, "Baby I need you"
Say, "Baby I can't [can not] live without you"

FUCK ME OUT OF MY NEGRO

The blood line Cherokee and Cheyenne

Had nothing but Negro men

Sitting on her pouch with snuff and tobacco in her mouth

Rising; rolling her eyes; going into the house

The woman is depicting a win

Saying to herself, under her breath, "I can"

Fuck me out of my Negro

Park your car in front of her front door

Saying, "Once more"

Fuck me out my Negro

Mating with a Cherokee and Sioux

She does not know the truth

Not having a husband of her own

Her mind becomes gone

Fuck me out of my Negro

She was born a whore

Her mother died before she reached four

Please, fuck me out of my Negro

Each and everyday a constant struggle

Everybody in town says she will buckle

Not able to fin on her own

She depends on assistance and many Toms
Trying to keep up a home
The story goes no mistakes told
As she grows old
A city of fools know of her mental abuse
This is to be true

Fuck me out of my Negro
Indian bloodline for sure
Mother Cherokee; Father Cheyenne
Negroid by the white man

Fuck me out my Negro
She will constantly pay for this
As she kiss ass and take bull shit

Once more...

Please, fuck me out of my Negro

SEVEN

The moon is just a hazing
The sun is just a blazing
But what is so amazing
Is my love for you
In the mist of a happy moment
In the bliss of happiness
I know that life is not a pretense

Seven days
Seven miles
Seven ways
I am my mother seventh child

People in a classroom
Learning a new skill
Rocking back forward as if they are mentally ill
Says to oneself, "She can not be for real"
As I take the telescope and sees how his heartbeat feels

Seven ways
Seven days
Seven miles
I am my mother seventh child
As intelligence and foolishness compiles

Verlena Sexton-Walker

The moon is hazing
The sun is blazing
What is so amazing
Is the love I have for you
In the mist of a happy moment
In the bliss of happiness
I know that life is not just a pretense
My time has been well spent

The seventh child of my mother
Have three sisters and two brothers
Drives down a seven mile road everyday
Has seven ways to say
I love you and believe in you in each and everyway

GORILLA

The man and cottonell
Outside my dining room window
Has a criminal demise in his ass
Thinking the hippness is recourse
This is not a chose
But only a damn fool lacking voice

Why do you do things that are uncool
As we claim something that is not ours
The ghetto; the hippest show belongs to no one
This is only done in fun
Entertainment once more

Again is to repeat
As he beat his meat
Thinking of sex that he will have
Why not wait for finally
Beating your meat only misleads
Enjoyment, release, and escape
Beating your meat is [not] the only way

Why do you do things that are uncool
As you claim something that is not ours
The ghetto; the hippest show belongs to no one
This is only done in fun
Entertainment once more
Don't exit out of the front door

The ghetto is said to be the way we act
Not a part of a city or town as a matter of fact
This is some people way of life
The hippest show is the way we represent
Was this sense borrow or lent
As the Negro white man begins to pant
Entertainment is well meant

"Apeness is in the making through the milieu of faking. The only
one whom is shaking is the one who is hating."
(Verlena Sexton-Walker)

PRO ATHLETES ANALOGIES

Justification of this rhyme is poetic and base on crime
Two goes into eleven five point five times

He is retarded
Not very smart
As he sits at my table with a penis that is hard
He masquerades around town as if he has it going on
This is all that is known

Pro athlete Vince Carter is in the room
Mentality of man no strength in the place
As I write what I see on this page
He will tell all that he does not know me
As if this poem is make believe
The dream is a machine

Lacking vision of a human being
He stands on a black TV screen
Saying, "This is my dream
To scheme to win
To shake each and every white man hand
To lie about facts
To make pretense that this is all an act
To be like India Arie

Who wants to be just like me
To walk like I am a proud criminal
As this dream continues to unfold

Pro Athlete Jerry Stackhouse is in the room
Mentality of man no strength in the place
As I write what I see on this page
He will tell all that he does not know me
As if this poem is make believe
If you hear me sing, I am not tired
If you hear me speak
I am not finish
If you say be quiet
I am winning

He swings the genitals on a towel
He says things out loud
I never know what to expect
This one is not pro best bet

Pro Athlete Michael Jordan is retired
He always call on the police
Can he not be a little more discreet
This is the end of this piece

As The Future Unfolds

This is a poem about an unkept identity

This is a poem about injustice

This is a poem about jealousy

This is a poem about atrocities against me

I am Native American

Victorious is the name

I fear no man

As they disguise themselves as missionaries

Incompetent to the theme

They continue to dream

In mentality of specialty

These men live in an idiosyncrasy

If you had a choose

Would you chose

If your voice count

Can you still lose

This is how fools continue to be used

This poetry expresses triumphs

This poetry expresses emotions

This poetry is not for old that does not age gracefully

This poetry is hatred of that who disrespects humanity

Verlena Sexton-Walker

If your chose was youth, would you be true
If your voice was wise, would you guide
This tells that when old overrides God
Claiming a victory is not very hard
Aging should not be a disregard
Playing young is not very smart

LET ME

I group
I cult
I am sister
I am brother
Never to know my mother
I am fatherless
When I see people harmonizing
I don't begin despicing
I know they lack intelligence

Let me is all he says
You let me is what he believes
This is how he is deceived

I have sex
I fuck
I make love
In the buck
As his dick hits the right stroke
I rise and began to smoke
Saying to him
Hmmm, "That was good"
As I stand; he stood

Let me; lacks meaning
Bet me; you will lose
This how I begin to depict this fool

I use lotion
Never grease
I see nothing but teeth
These men misleads
People believe that he will win
This should be his end

Let me is bad terminology
It lacks creativity
Only a coward would ask for that
This is how the man fights
Let me is the bullet in his back

Amanda

I am my own hero
I have no idol or role model
This will ensure me certain greatness
As I travel this journey in life
That which gives me strength to fight

A wise man and two little ones sits by a pond
He begins to talk of a fable with a moral
This is the story he tells...

There was a baby long ago who parents abandon her
They left her in the woods all along for only a second
When they came back from getting wood, she was gone
They never found her
As time past this child stayed in a certain mentality
She was breeded by apelike people and given a certain humanity
Thirty years later humans came upon this vessel in the forest in
which they discovered these apelike people
This girl name was Ama that humans mistook for Amanda
They (humans) kidnapped this girl
Took her from her apelike family where they made her into a
Princess Diana
Taught her how to speak fluent English and she sang beautifully
This girl was overlooked in history

Verlena Sexton-Walker

I am heroic
I am impression
I am what man call a manifestation
In all I am no more than you
This is not misleading but to be true
I am Amanda, a prisoner of war, and I do what I have to do

INTRO TO CRIMINAL JUSTICE

I know a fitty bitch

His dick is not worth shit

His initials is J.S.

He study put me to the test

Follow me to class

As if he wants to whip my ass

He trenscends through my floor

He comes in my backdoor

This fitty bitch says, "Lets show her"

With the ending being her know

This fitty bitch has to go

SPECIES TO SPECIMEN

I wonder why we continue to kill
Do men really not feel
The thrust of the atomic bomb that rise
       from the dust
How much do we have to hurt
Never showing emotions of lost
Pain is our enemy
Telling us that we are victorious
As we kill a certain spiritual humanity
      (mentality)

Unben the spoon man and let the fork
      have its run
The poem will than flow and give message
      to everyone
Release the pain in one loud shout
This poem is meaning of life itself
Never let the spoon ben again
The fork has to walk
Creating an opening of joy forever more

Ghetto to a bum is a Barbershop rerun
Running around at midnight
With a dorag on instead of a cap
Feels his life will change
Holds up another Negro man
Forgetting where this would take his life

to
He shots the Negro and in African slang
    "He flew"
Caught by the police
He is arraign with a prison sentence
Life changing drastically
This Negro feels certain victory

When you meet this whore
Did she approach you
Or did she give you a wedding ban
This whore loved you
In an immensely way
She just didn't want you to be another
    trip in the hay
However, you feel; you missed out on many
    good fucks
Now it is how to get a 'great' dick suck

The Moon and Venus becomes one
The passion left is her spent
In the arms of a windless breath
Venus surrounds this Greek Island
    impatiently
This is to be her tieranny
As her hair still blows freely
The moon regains its pedestal
Memory of yesterday is reclaimed

Verlena Sexton-Walker

Venus is the Greek Island name
Depicting a senseless shame

I wonder why we continue to kill
Do men really feel
The thrust of the atomic bomb that rise
        from the dust
How much do we have to hurt
Never showing emotions of lost
Pain is our enemy
Telling us that we are victorious
As we kill to glory us

        ****

If any moral is told this is a message by
        far and to be true
Don't go to War... Let War come to you

LISTENING TO LEADERS THAT FOLLOWS THE GREAT DIVIDED

The shoes are statement of priority
Snuffing those who can not see
That jellies beans are in the destiny
Or a fashion that never leaves
But proceeds through ignorancy
If I was my brother and my brother was me
He would lack cognitive to see
That it was his destiny to be a man
Wearing my shoes does not change things

The great divided can be many things
A man giving you a wedding ring
Is his love false of really true
This can make you blue
Unable to grasp what it means
Asking yourself, "Do I love him enough or is he a friend
                    forever more"

What if you can not pretend
What if the voices are in the wind
What if these young men
Say that old pussy is all that is in
Screaming while lying on their backs
As they lick shit out of ass cracks
These young men dreams of reincarnation of MLKing

Jr. on the end

This is how they depicts a win

With Louis Farrakan at the dining room window

Saying, "Is this another Civil Rights Movement"

Malcolm X standing in New York for food stamps and the

house

All is sickness of past as a woman continue to whip their

ass

Through a mentality of old

These fools have been told

As an ending unfolds

If suicide was a chose

Can we find another recourse

As we stick a needle in our arm

As we shot ourselves in the head with a gun

Once suicide is chosen

There is no turning back

On the night of suicide

We forget where we are at

Exhaling our last breath

God does forgive - for goodness has left

But loneliness only comes when we are together

Sitting at the table daydreaming

Such a lonesome fellow

Not compatible to each

No conversation lack of poetic

This loneliness can become pathetic

To acquire a more deeper gift

This loneliness grows you up

This woman had to many men for one
She open her legs on every turn
Never feeling shameful or disgrace
She continue to deceive men each and everyday
Too many for one
Too much for some
This woman seem to lack none
In all she gave, a provision was made
This woman knew how to get laid
Dreaming, she turns to the opposite
A man lies between her legs
She mourns in ecstasy
And expression of joy
This woman has not went to far
Loving herself sexually erotic her
The hypno trace of bliss
This woman rise putting his dick in her first
Bringing it to her mouth
She moves her head horizontally
This woman knows she will succeed
This man joy explodes all at once
He ejaculates
This woman proceeds to the next
Too many for one
Is unreal...
Not having her is not possible

This woman goes from man to the simple school boy

The vagina must he the asshole that you smell
It reversed itself said Ruleville
However, it changes into a fangot dick
The vagina of Michael Jordan smell like a bitch
He puts his face behind the one he talks about
His vagina should be cut out
The vagina of a bitch is in the house
Saying, "You are the nobody that ruin me"
This stink box is the dick between his teeth

Bastards write how bastards sees
The world bastards are usually misleads
AIDS is a fatal disease
Why do bastards always read
This world peace only helps bastards to breed
Not only a damn shame but a false deed
Claim only your proceeds

The great divided can be many things
A man giving you a engagement ring
Is his love false or true
This can make you blue
Unable to grasp what it means
Asking yourself, "Do I love him enough or is he a friend
                    forever more"
As you analyze while closing your bedroom door

THE STARS

If the wind blows

If the rain pours

If the chair unfold

I stand alone

Not with anyone

The sound on my roof

The slamming of the door

The frigid cold

Fragile as glass

By pass but not last

One star is strength

Two stars – "What is meant?"

Three stars – Life line kept

Four stars – Depicts a win

Five stars – The idiosyncrasy of man

Noise is salient

Voices are silent

The music of a pleasant scent

I stand alone

Not with anyone

The wind blows loud

In the face of a cloud

The open of the door

Verlena Sexton-Walker

Closes to life manifold
Delicate to the touch
Much – Too Much

1 star is expressions unheard
2 stars - You are the world
3 stars – Speak forever more
4 stars – "Who do you think you are?"
5 stars – "Why try so hard?"
Dancing in the sun

One star is alone
Two stars is not one
Three stars is a beginning
Four stars - Has no ending
Five stars - What a pity

Amazing Grace

Why do women want to be mental man

Because they are not strong enough

Or - Maybe they are to strong

Who knows

The story goes

Harriet Tubman freed slaves by way of the Underground Railroad

In rackety clothes, she did this until she became old

Many women raise their children with little money while they man

implant another

The struggle is a continuous toll as femininity sees masculinity

folds

A personality discrepancy is known when a man manhood is not

shown

In the life of many women the man can be a hinderance

Wanting them to submit in their shadows'

The man is nothing but a low-life ignorant coward

Money becomes prevalent

As he lacks intelligence to do anything else

Why do women want to be mental men

Lack of strength

Or - strength seen {within}

Do you know

Many stories can be told...

THE PROOF IS IN THE PUTTING (BURDEN OF PROOF)

Some people know that they are not a factual reality
Some people know that they are in a mentality
Many times they can not look you directly in the eyes
This is how they lie...

I am a prophecy
I am the personification of history
There are many movements in me
This is my identity
I hate those that see my transparency
My name is within the mind
I depict each and everyone's time
Their life line should be mine
Why do I live through others lives
Because I despice mine?
A woman life is the life I am trying to claim
This will give me certain fame
As the ass is my aim
Flipping this game
I have no shame
Her name should be mine
As she sees me putting my dick in an old man's behind
The thing is she is older than me
She is not easily deceive

As I believe this is my victory
A mission I was called for
The world I will retard
My dick stays hard
I show it to every girl and boy
Belittle myself
Straight jacket
Hand cuffed
This is not enough
I must claim her identity
She is to much for me
Victorious is definitely her victory?
As this story unfolds...
Let's wait and see

WIERDO

This dick in my fist is a self-destruction stance

If I ever get the chance, I will rape a man

My sexual identity is homosexuality

I stand in ignorancy

Because no man wants me

My head is bald

I am 6'6', not very tall

I lend when I walk

I talk with a slur

Stuttering as you heard

I love to play sports

Basketball by choice

This is because it is my only voice

Rapping my forte

I run words together anyway

I hate being played

This is my key to getting laid

Maybe I will go pro

Cow Polk I will not know

This is not a show

Before I get old

The world will know my crimes

I am jealous of any woman that can rhyme

This is my very last line

Why...

I'm out of time.

About The Author

Being a published author of poetry and prose, a spiritual healer, and a teacher, expression in words are an important part of my life. As an author, expression in words can bring about sensitivity, creativity, and captivate the mind completely. This captivation of words can spiritually heal a person's inner (spiritual) being as well as well as his/her mental you (the mind). This teaches one that expression must be done through our mind to convey to others and ourselves. All are important gifts/assets in my life; provide strength to me as a writer, teacher, and spiritual healer; and can give insurmountable benefits to any individual or group that seeks a blessing and/or lesson in life through the eloquence of words.

Verlena Sexton-Walker, BSCJ - BSSS - MBAGM

05/10/2004

Note: Let it be known that the Bachelor of Science in Criminal Justice (BSCJ); the Bachelor of Science in Social Sciences (BSSS); and the Master Of Business Administration and Global Management (MBAGM) are degrees acquire and held by Verlena Sexton-Walker.

www.ingramcontent.com/pod-product-compliance
Lightning Source LLC
Chambersburg PA
CBHW020341290526
45785CB00005B/2127